Combat Sports

BY MATT DOEDEN

D0907943

AMICUS HIGH INTEREST ✦ AMICUS INK

Amicus High Interest and Amicus Ink are imprints of Amicus
P.O. Box 1329, Mankato, MN 56002
www.amicuspublishing.us

Library of Congress Cataloging-in-Publication Data
Doeden, Matt.
 Combat sports / by Matt Doeden.
    pages cm. – (Summer Olympic sports)
 Includes index.
 Summary: "Presents information about the rules and types of
combat sports in the Olympics, including wrestling, boxing, tae
kwon do, judo, and fencing"– Provided by publisher.
 ISBN 978-1-60753-807-3 (library binding)
 ISBN 978-1-60753-896-7 (ebook)
 ISBN 978-1-68152-048-3 (paperback)
 1. Wrestling–Juvenile literature. 2. Boxing–Juvenile literature.
 3. Martial arts–Juvenile literature. 4. Fencing–Juvenile
literature. 5. Olympics–Juvenile literature. I. Title.
 GV1195.3.D64 2016
 796.8–dc23

                        2014045773

Editor: Wendy Dieker
Series Designer: Kathleen Petelinsek
Book Designer: Aubrey Harper
Photo Researcher: Derek Brown

Photo Credits: ORESTIS PANAGIOTOU/epa/Corbis
cover; Daiju Kitamura/AFLO/Nippon News/Corbis 5; Paul
Cunningham/Corbis 6; Paul Sancya/ /AP/Corbis 8-9; Daiju
Kitamura/AFLO/Nippon News/Corbis 10; Scott Heavey/
Getty Images 13; JOHN G. MABANGLO/epa/Corbis 14;
Liu Dawei/xh/Xinhua Press/Corbis 17; Clifford White/Corbis
18; Alexander Hassenstein/Getty Images 21; KIM KYUNG-
HOON/Reuters/Corbis 22; DOMINIC EBENBICHLER/
Reuters/Corbis 25; SERGEI ILNITSKY/epa/Corbis 26;
ANDREW MILLS/Star Ledger/Corbis 28-29

Printed in Malaysia

HC 10 9 8 7 6 5 4 3 2 1
PB 10 9 8 7 6 5 4 3 2 1

Table of Contents

Going for Gold

The athletes. The drama. The glory. There's nothing else like the Olympics. It happens every four years. Athletes put on one of the greatest shows in sport. They all share one dream: a gold medal.

Combat sports have always been part of the games. They are tests of strength, skill, and will.

 When was the first Olympic Games?

Japanese wrestler Kaori Icho shows off the gold medal she won in the 2012 Olympics.

 The very first Olympics was held in Greece. It was 776 B.C. But the games we know today started in 1896.

Women have been wrestling each other at the Olympics since 2004.

 Which nation has the most Olympic wrestling medals?

Wrestling

Two wrestlers step onto the mat. The match begins. The wrestlers circle each other. One strikes! She takes down the other woman. She **pins** her to the mat! This is wrestling. It was one of the first Olympic sports. The sport has changed a lot. But the basics are the same. Wrestlers use strength and power to win the match.

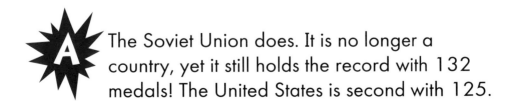
The Soviet Union does. It is no longer a country, yet it still holds the record with 132 medals! The United States is second with 125.

Two kinds of wrestling take place at the Olympics. One kind is freestyle. There are matches for men and women. They can use their arms or legs to make a **hold**.

Men can also compete in Greco-Roman wrestling. This style is more like the ancient sport. Wrestlers can use only their arms and upper bodies for holds.

These men wrestle for a bronze medal in the 2012 Olympics.

Ryutaro Matsumoto from Japan takes down his opponent in the 2012 Olympics.

 Q What happens if no one gets pinned?

Wrestlers come in all sizes. But they take on only wrestlers of the same size. The smallest athletes are in the flyweight class. The biggest ones are the super heavyweights.

Athletes wrestle for two periods. They are three minutes long. The match ends if a wrestler pins his or her opponent.

 Wrestlers get points for taking their opponent down. Escapes from holds also earn points. The wrestler with the most points wins.

Boxing

Dodge! Weave! Punch! Olympic boxing has always been a hit. Today, both men and women face off in the ring. They go toe-to-toe in three or four rounds. Rounds are two or three minutes long. Boxers earn points in each round. They can score by landing lots of softer punches. A few big ones get higher scores.

Olympic boxers wear big padded gloves and helmets.

A boxer lands a big punch
in the gold-medal match
in the 2008 Olympics.

Matches don't always go to the end of the round. They sometimes end with a **knockout**. That's when a boxer gets punched hard and falls to the mat. If the **ref** counts to ten, the match is over.

Weight classes keep fights even. Men battle it out in ten classes. Women have three. The top two boxers in each class fight for the gold medal.

Martial Arts

The fighters bow to each other. And then they kick! Tae kwon do is a **martial art** from South Korea. Men and women thrill fans with fights that include big kicks. It can be a dangerous sport. Athletes must wear pads on the head and body. Guards protect the shins and forearms.

Tae kwon do means "the way of the fist and foot." The feet are what score points.

Fighters wear helmets and pads to stay safe.

 How are kicks counted?

In tae kwon do, not all kicks are equal. Each kick has a point value. Straight kicks to the body are worth 1 point. A straight kick to the head is worth 3 points. Spinning kicks are worth 2 points to the body and 4 points to the head.

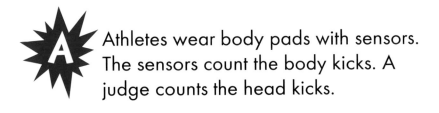

Athletes wear body pads with sensors. The sensors count the body kicks. A judge counts the head kicks.

On another mat, two judo fighters bow to each other. They have no pads. The ref starts the match. One athlete grabs the other. They **grapple**. They throw each other around. This martial art is called "the gentle way." Fighters don't score points by punching or kicking. Instead, they use holds and throws.

 Why is judo called "the gentle way"?

Judo is about control and strength. Fighters do not punch or kick.

 Judo students learn to fight without weapons or strikes. They use balance and strength instead.

South Korean fighter Wang Ki-Chun throws his opponent to the mat.

 What happens if no one scores an ippon?

The goal in a judo match is to score an ippon. This is a throw that lands an opponent on his or her back. An ippon ends the match. A match can also end by a submission. This is when one fighter is in a painful hold and gives up.

The match ends after 5 minutes. Judges score the match based on the throws.

Fencing

Slash! Thrust! Dodge! Fencing is the sword fighting of today. Men and women compete in three different fencing events. They are foil, épée, and saber. Each event is named for the sword used. All three swords are light and thin. The foil and épée have a button on the end. The saber does not.

Foil fencers use the end of
the sword to touch their
opponent's vest.

Masks and vests have sensors that light up when the sword touches them.

 Q Is fencing dangerous?

The fencers attack with great speed. They block attacks with quick flicks of the wrist. Fencers earn points for touching their opponent's body. In foil and épée, the end of the sword must touch the fighter. In saber, fencers can use the edge of the swords for touches. The fencer with the most points wins.

 It can be. Fencers have been badly hurt. But injuries are rare. Today, protective clothes and masks help keep fencers safe.

Bring on the Olympics!

Combat athletes train hard for the biggest fight of their lives. Whether you like boxing or martial arts, swords or wrestling, you will have fun watching the Olympics. So sit back and enjoy! Cheer on your favorite athletes as they go for the gold!

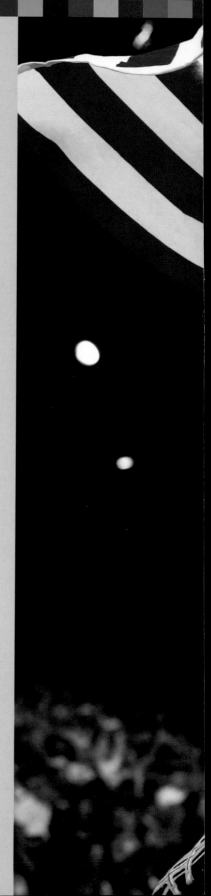

Freestyle wrestler Jordan Burroughs celebrates his win in 2012.

Glossary

grapple To grab an opponent and try to make a hold or pin while avoiding getting held or pinned by an opponent.

hold In wrestling and judo, a way of stopping an opponent from moving and attacking.

ippon In judo, a move to throw an opponent to the mat; an ippon ends the match.

knockout In boxing, a punch that knocks an opponent unconscious; a knockout ends the match.

martial art A kind of fighting that originated as a form of self-defense.

pin In wrestling, to force an opponent's back flat against the mat.

ref Short for referee; the person who judges a match and makes sure the rules are followed.

Read More

Butterfield, Moira. *The Olympics: Events.* Mankato, Minn.: Sea-to-Sea Publications, 2012.

Hunter, Nick. *The 2012 London Olympics.* Chicago: Heinemann, 2012.

Peters, Stephanie True. *Great Moments in the Summer Olympics.* New York: Little, Brown and Co. 2012.

Websites

BBC Primary History—The Olympic Games
http://www.bbc.co.uk/schools/primaryhistory/ancient_greeks/the_olympic_games/

How Fencing Equipment Works
http://entertainment.howstuffworks.com/fencing-equipment.htm

Official Site of the Olympic Movement
http://www.olympic.org/

Index

About the Author

Author and editor Matt Doeden has written hundreds of children's and young adult books. Some of his books have been listed among the Best Children's Books of the Year by the Children's Book Committee at Bank Street College. Doeden lives in Minnesota with his wife and two children.